Adventures In Teaching

A Guide To Becoming An English Teacher Abroad

DAVID ZELNAR

DEDICATION

For my parents. Without your support, I would have never been able to go on these adventures and see the world. You are the ones who taught me to fly.

CONTENTS

ACKNOWLEDGMENTS

First of all I would like to thank my parents, who supported me in chasing my dreams. I would like to thank my brother Zachary for joining me on my first trip abroad and helping me find my sense of adventure. I would also like to thank Neil Bennion for encouraging me to write this book and assisting me through the entire process. Also, Nate Bloemke and the University of Florida English Language Institute for giving me my first job teaching English as a Language Assistant. Special thanks to all the schools around the world who gave me the opportunity to teach and the students who made the job enjoyable. Also a special thanks to all my family and friends who encouraged me along the way.

1 INTRODUCTION

The first time I moved abroad I was petrified. I had done a bit of traveling before in Central America, but that was a vacation. This time I was staying without a return ticket home. I got off the bus from Bangkok and arrived in the small village where I was to spend the next couple months before I moved to my more permanent post. Standing there, mid afternoon, with my luggage at my side, on the steps of a local high school, waiting for my only local contact to pick me up, I felt the pit of my stomach begin to swell. A small white car pulls up; an older Thai woman steps out and says, "Are you David?" All I could do was nod my head as she helped me load my car. "You stay at my sister place." I just continued to nod; I could tell that she saw the fear in my eyes.

We took my things to my new "home",

standing outside was a slightly older, bald American man wearing a Kansas Jayhawks baseball jersey. At this point I was shaking. My stomach wrenched itself into knots. I didn't know if I was going to faint or vomit. He looked at me and laughed, "First time living abroad, huh?" I nodded. "Alright then, are you ready for your tour of the town?" he gestures towards his quite large motorcycle. I told him I needed a minute, as I continued my nervous chain smoking. I thought to myself, relax, this is what you wanted. This is your adventure.

Brahrrrr…..pampapapampa. The motorcycle roars to life. Either of us without a helmet, I climb onto the back. In a flash we were off, my heart now to the point of near collapse. I've been on motorcycles before, but now I'm on the back of one zipping through a small Thai village with a total stranger and we're on the opposite side of the road. He's pointing and explaining where things are and showing me landmarks. All I can think is I'm going to die my first day here on this damn motorcycle.

Flash-forward to today and now I am able to pack up and move to a new country without any hesitation. The pit in my stomach no longer takes residence. The fear is gone. I now have experience, am certified, and am highly employable. I moved to Europe with no job leads and within a month I was able to have my pick of employment. I now have the ability to travel to just about any country and have the confidence that I will find work. But, I would not be able to do any of this without first having the courage to take that initial position as an English teacher in a small village in Thailand.

2 WHAT IS TEACHING ENGLISH AS A FOREIGN LANGUAGE?

Teaching English as a foreign language or TEFL is different than teaching English to native speakers. It is the development of language skills for non-native speakers. Native speakers are typically hired for our speaking ability. The students are able to practice with someone who speaks the language naturally. The best listening/speaking exercises are done with native speakers, because we don't have to process the language like a person whom English is a second language. Base grammar knowledge is also essential for a TEFL teacher. One does not need to be an expert in grammar to become a TEFL teacher, but the more knowledge one has in the subject the more effective and successful he or she will be. You can always brush up on your grammar skills while you are preparing for the lesson, but make sure you understand the concept completely because the students will expect you to be able to answer their questions. Many TEFL certificate courses offer grammar courses if you feel you want to increase your skill in a more formal setting.

There are many different types of TEFL teaching jobs. You can teach toddlers, children, teenagers, university students, adults, business English, or job specific learning. You should decide which level you prefer and what skill sets you bring. I have taught in each of the levels and I personally prefer higher level and adult courses, not to say I haven't enjoyed teaching children as well. Many private schools will have you teach at several different levels, but you should try and decide what you prefer. If you are not a kid person, I would not suggest teaching at a primary school.

Teaching English as a foreign language can be a demanding profession. It is up to you though how much you want to work. I will discuss the different types of schools and jobs in more detail in a later section. It is a job that you should prepare for every day and dedicate time away from work for planning and grading. Teachers get to work while off the clock, fun right. But, even though it can be a demanding job and should be taken seriously (many people go overseas and are horrible teachers, because they don't take the job seriously and haphazardly wing their lessons) it can be the most rewarding job in the world. You get out of it the same that you put into it.

3 COMMON MISCONCEPTIONS

Many people have misconceptions about Teaching English as a Foreign Language. For example, many people think that they can teach with no experience and no qualifications because they are a native speaker and already know the language. Just because you can speak a language does not mean that you can teach it. You can find a job without any qualifications, experience, or certifications but that does not mean that you will be an effective teacher.

Many people feel that they can just walk into a classroom and have general conversations about subjects and that will be enough for the students. Whereas conversation classes are important and are primarily what native speakers are hired for, you need to put more into your lessons than just talking about random subjects. You need a reason for having these conversations. For example: if you decide to have a conversation class about travel, make the objective of the class to use "would like", "have been", and past and future tenses.

This is why I suggest doing a TEFL course. These courses will help you organize your lesson plans and make the classroom experience better for you and your students. It will show you how to structure a class and how to handle certain issues. These courses not only pad your resume with a certificate, they give you experience and help you understand what the job requires. If you have never taught before, do not go into this profession thinking you are an expert. Be willing to learn and grow as a teacher and the job will come much easier.

4 CAN I DO THIS?

Now this part is up to you. But in short, yes you can. All you need to do is figure out what qualifications you need and where you want to go. A lot of times you can contact the school well in advance and begin discussing what qualifications you are going to need before you head over. A school in Turkey showed me what minimum certificate they required and where I could get certified for low cost after my initial interview. We stayed in touch while I took the online courses and had the follow up interview upon completion. Funny thing is, I ended up moving to Poland and working for a completely different company.

If time away is your concern, don't let it be. There are summer camps, positions for single semesters, as well as long term contracts. How long you live overseas is up to you. Remember, just because you are under contract does not mean that you can't leave if you feel uneasy and want to go home. If you cut the contract short, the only repercussion will be that that school or company probably won't hire you again. You hold the power and can choose how long you plan on living overseas. I will say this though, if you make a commitment to a company or school, try to make it the full length of the contract to be fair to the students, so they are not in a constant merry-go-round of teachers. Only leave if you are absolutely unhappy or have to.

This is your adventure. Take the reigns and see places that you have always wanted to and be part of a different culture for a while. Anyone can go on vacation, but you are going to do so much more. Do not let minor fears hold you back. As I said before, you can go home any time you want to. Take the first step and explore the world of endless possibilities. The world is under your terms, now join the ranks of teachers abroad and prepare to share in something amazing.

5 WHY WOULD I DO THIS?

If you are hesitant and the idea of leaving your friends and family and living in another country frightens you, then congratulations you are normal. This is going to be a scary experience, especially if you do it alone. If you can find a friend who is willing to go on this adventure with you, then you are lucky and might have an easier transition phase. But I promise you, the reward of teaching abroad outweighs the risk a thousand fold. I have done some traveling and seen some amazing places, but on these trips I am always an outsider looking in. When you live and work abroad, you get to be part of the culture and gain an understanding of the people you live among.

You begin to make local friends and enjoy local customs. You will celebrate their holidays and cheer for their teams. You will go to places that your average tourist will never have heard of. You become one of them. Now it is impossible to become fully integrated into another society; but when you come home, you will catch yourself continuing to follow the new customs. I bowed for the first month after returning from Asia.

You will also begin to see the amazing similarities that your culture shares with you new home. A place that before arrival seems so distant and different will play your favorite song on the radio. There are also plenty of people living abroad and they normally meet up on a regular basis. You can easily find them on Facebook or other social media sites. A word of caution: do not just hang out with expats (Ex-patriots are people who have left their country and live abroad). They can be a comfort and give you a piece of home in a foreign land. Also, if they speak the same language it makes communication easier. But, it's always good to make local friends. People will want to be your friend just because you are foreign and they want to work on their English. You will get the full experience of a culture if you spend time with the people. I have seen people who end up only hanging out with other foreigners and they remain a tourist their entire stay. Become a local, or try to be as much as possible.

6 PICK A COUNTRY

So, you're ready to go. But, where are you going? It's a huge world out there and as an ESL (English as a Second Language) teacher your options are endless. Obviously countries whose primary language is English are not on this list. This is when you need to think of what you are looking for in your adventure. But, you may be surprised at where you end up. I was looking for a job in Europe and ended up in Thailand, and another time I was looking for jobs in the Emirates and ended up in Poland. So, it depends on what you are looking for; me, I just wanted an adventure and did not care where I went.

Now, if you are looking for the highest paying jobs then northern Asia (China, Korea, Japan) and the Middle East are the best bet. You can find decent paying jobs throughout the world, but you need to remember to base the salary on the cost of living in that country and not your own. The equivalent of a thousand dollars a month may not be a lot in your country, but in some countries you can live quite well. The Middle East (Kuwait, Qatar, Saudi Arabia, United Arab Emirates, etc.) tends to pay the most, but because of this they have the most competition for the job. Northern Asia on the other hand pays well and is always looking for native speakers; there is no job shortage in this region. Europe is also an option for decent paying jobs, but the farther east you go the easier it is to find a job as a new teacher. South America and Africa are still options out there, but majority of the postings I have seen are low paying; not to say that you cannot find a job in one of these countries that is sustainable. Pay is typically reflective of the development of a nation.

7 HOW DO I FIND A JOB?

So, how do I find a job? I find that the best option is primarily online. I would suggest finding the job online as far in advance as possible. This way you have more time to prepare financially and end up with the job that you want. There are many online options out there. If you have a certain country in mind, it can be as simple as typing "ESL jobs in *insert country name*" into a search engine. You will mostly find job posting boards and some may require you to create an account. This is fine, as long as it is for free. There are many sites out there that are trying to scam people into paying for nothing. Remember you are what they are looking for; and if you would not pay to apply in your country, why would you do it for a job abroad?

There are also many job postings for ESL teaching or similar positions that span multiple countries. I prefer sites like this, because it gives you variety and comparative options. Although there are many ESL job-posting sites, I prefer to use Dave's ESL Cafe (www.eslcafe.com) for my job-hunting needs. This site in particular (other sites will have this as well) allows you to create a free profile with your curriculum vitae (CV) attached. This is great because employers can find you while you are looking as well. They can check out your CV and send you an interview request, and at the same time you have your CV and profile already set up to send to your employer. The only thing that you have to alter or create is a semi-optional cover letter, which I will discuss in a later section.

There are some of you that would prefer to simply move to a country and go on the job hunt in person. It is possible to move to a country on a tourist visa and look for work in person, but you must be financially prepared to sustain yourself while job hunting and for roughly a month after finding a job to receive your first paycheck. The country you decide to move to will have an effect on how difficult it will be to find a job in person. In some countries, it is quite easy to find a job as a native English teacher, especially if you have a TEFL certificate. But, some countries may have a flooded market and might be difficult to find work as a teacher, you should do some research before making this move.

The best way to search for possible employers is

through job portals. A simple URL search for "TEFL jobs in *insert country name*" can find you possible positions, you can decide if you want to go city specific or not. You can also do the job search in person. Language schools are typically the best route to go. They are easy to find and welcome teachers as applicants, especially native speakers. You can also try local universities, if you feel that you have the qualifications, but they do typically tend to hire people with experience. When going to schools in person and delivering your CV, it is best to do this mid-morning. You want to allow them time to set up for the day. If it is a language school, their busiest times are in the afternoon, because people take classes after work or school. Do not go there in the afternoon, they will not have time for you and your CV could be lost in the shuffle.

On the plus side, being in country makes you readily available for the employer and allows you to see first hand what kind of school you would be working at prior to making a commitment. One of the downfalls to applying online is that you are basing everything you know about a place or school on pictures and word of mouth. Being in country gives you the opportunity to see for yourself if you would want to live in that city. It also permits you the opportunity to "interview" possible employers while being interviewed yourself. You will be able to choose the job you feel is best suited. But, as I have stated before, do not undertake this expedition unless you can afford it, because it is uncertain when you will begin work and have a steady income.

8 WHAT QUALIFICATIONS DO I NEED?

Education

The subject of your degree does not typically matter if you are a native English speaker. Although, having a degree in Education or a similar field is always a plus and may even offer you more opportunities and higher paying jobs. If you are a speaker of English as a second language a degree in English, English Philology, or a similar field may be required.

Is it still possible to find a job as an ESL teacher if I do not have a degree? Yes it most definitely is. You do not need a degree to teach English overseas. You still have the advantage of being a native speaker. But, keep in mind that some jobs will require a degree, so be prepared for this issue. You will most likely need a TEFL certificate, which I will go into more detail about in the next section, and you should stress this certificate and your prior work experience in place of your education.

TEFL / CELTA Certificate

So what is a TEFL certificate or a CELTA? A TEFL or Teaching English as a Foreign Language certificate is qualifying proof that you understand how to teach the subject. The TEFL certificates range in hours and are based on how qualified you want to present yourself. If you have a degree and maybe some teaching experience, then the basic TEFL certificate is all you need. The more hours of a certificate that you take the more qualified you will become and the more you increase your chances of getting better employment. The CELTA or Certificate in English Language Teaching to Speakers of Other Languages is the most recognized and preferred certificate; because of this it is in turn the most expensive.

You should take into consideration what type of jobs you are looking for and your own personal budget when deciding on a certificate. Remember you can always add onto your certificate more hours and achieve a higher level of completion. Also, you can discuss the certificate with your potential employer and obtain the specific certificate that the school or their government requires of an ESL teacher.

If you are applying and you do not have a university degree, I would suggest getting the CELTA. It is the premier certificate out there and will strengthen your CV. Yet, I have met people without degrees that only had the basic TEFL certificate and were able to find work overseas. The main thing is you may be limited to certain regions and certain countries with less stringent requirements like Southeast Asia or Central America. I have been to both and would still highly recommend going to these regions.

How do I get a TEFL/ CELTA Certificate?

So where do I find a TEFL or CELTA certificate? Once again you can find these online. When you find a certificate online, make sure to research its source before paying for it. There are many options out there and some of them are not as credible as others. If you are on a budget, you can find several out there for a reasonable price. I have seen basic TEFL certificates for around 150 Euros/ 110 British Pounds/ 170 US Dollars. Keep in mind these values are equivalent with the exchange rate at the time of writing this and may change. I received my certificate through www.tefl.org.uk , it was relatively cheap and I have had no problems with an employer accepting it.

The online TEFL course can be completed in a relatively short time. They are offered in different hour segments. You can find work with the shortest one, but if you have time and want to make your CV stronger than going with more hours would be a good option. Many of these online TEFL course companies also offer grammar courses, which may be helpful if you are a little rusty on your grammatical skills.

The typical TEFL course will be a series of videos or readings followed by a short test, that you can take as many times as needed. Every few chapters, you will be asked to submit a situational response of how you would teach a certain lesson or react to a certain situation. They most likely will have a person designated to you who will grade these responses. This person is also there to answer any questions you may have and help you through the certificate, so do not be afraid to contact this person. They tend to be very friendly and helpful. Upon completion you will receive a digital copy and a copy by post of your certificate. Some schools will want to see this so make sure to have access to it.

If you want to be safe, go with the highest credited certificates or a CELTA certificate; but as I have mentioned before, discussing this with your potential employer first is a good route to take and you are guaranteed to have the necessary requirements.

The intensive CELTA TEFL course was one of the most challenging four weeks of my life – but also one of the most rewarding. The course was absolutely full on, including giving the first class on just the second or third day. Every day was packed full of teaching, observing, peer group feedback, learning about English language, learning how to teach and so on. The evenings offered no respite, as it typically took 4 or more hours each night to prepare the next day's class, including creating a full lesson plan. And that's without even mentioning the coursework. It was insane, and pretty much everyone was on the verge of quitting at some point. But we all supported one another – the sense of solidarity alone was great – and everybody pulled through. Come the end of it all, everyone was able to pore excitedly over job offers, knowing that not only could they teach in theory, they could also teach in practice (not to mention in Korea, Chile, Slovakia and so on). Yes, it's expensive, but for me, at least, it was absolutely worth it. – Neil Bennion

There are schools in many countries where you can earn a TEFL certificate, but these are usually not well accredited and are only useful in that particular country. There are exceptions to this, so research a school before enrolling and make sure that it is accredited with an internationally recognized organization. You may also be able to find certificate courses available in your home country as well. If you are able to go to Canada, the University of Toronto offers a great program.

9 TYPES OF SCHOOLS

There are primarily three different types of schools out there: government, private, and language. The type of school is something you should take into consideration when looking for a job. The type of school will impact pay rate, visa status, working hours, and what is expected from you. You should also take into consideration the age group you prefer to teach. If you are more comfortable with adults, then a primary school is probably not for you and vice versa.

Government schools are typically the most structured. They will most likely be salary based and consistent with their pay. Your schedule will not be flexible. They will have a set number of classes and you will be expected to have your students meet certain requirements. In some countries they have a state issued exam, whereas others will require you to submit a final to be approved. You are expected to be there every day and your hours are similar to those of schools back home. Depending on the country your classes may be larger at these schools. Think of any foreign language classes that you have had in school and this is what they expect abroad; they are just fortunate to have a native speaker.

Private schools may have a similar set up as government schools: similar hours, etc. The difference is that this is private funded, so the students tend to be from a more elevated economic background. The class sizes may also be smaller than the government schools. This also leaves the chance that the pay rate might also be increased in comparison to government schools, but is not always the case. Some governments pay foreign teachers more and offer more benefits in order to have native speakers in their schools. In the private sector you will have varied types of schools as well. It may just be a privatized school, a bilingual school, or an English speaking school. In most private schools you will most likely be a TEFL teacher to local students. In a bilingual school you will be teaching local students, but they also take their other subjects in English. An English speaking school is primarily for native speaking students whose parents live abroad. There can still be local students whose parents prefer their child's education be in English.

Language schools are some of the most

common jobs available out there. These jobs are very flexible and allow you to work as much or as little as you want. One issue with these types of jobs is that you typically have to pay for your own visa and receive only limited assistance in this matter. These schools offer an hourly wage, which is normally well above the national average. These schools are also not as structured as the government or private schools. Each one of your classes will vary and you will need to mold the curriculum to the student or students. At these schools you will have small class sizes and most likely individual courses as well. The schedule will be in a constant flux and is tailored to the student's need. On the bright side, there are not normally too many early morning classes.

Another option is working at colleges or universities. These jobs tend to pay the highest, but are the most demanding. They are also the most selective when it comes to candidates. Many colleges and universities require the teacher to have a Master's degree or a Bachelor's degree in Education, English, or a similar field. It is possible to get a job with a degree in a different subject, but it depends on the college or university and their needs. If you do not possess a degree, then these jobs will be difficult to obtain. They also tend to hire teachers with experience and will ask for you to make a curriculum or syllabus in advance.

There are also volunteer teaching organizations

available around the world. These are the easiest to qualify for, but are typically unpaid or low paying. Many of these jobs do provide you with food and shelter. They tend to be in underdeveloped, impoverished, or remote regions of the world. This is a great way to give back and experience a place that few have the chance to visit. The students are excited to learn and you have the opportunity make a positive impact on their lives. If experience is more important to you than income, then this is a great option.

Agents

Now, there are agencies out there that recruit teachers for schools. Personally, I would try and steer clear of these companies. They can be useful in the aspect that they know what schools are looking for teachers and they are typically native English speakers themselves. But, remember what's good for them isn't necessarily good for you; they're looking after their own interest. With this in mind, going through an agent has its downfalls. You may not end up where you originally planned. They also might misrepresent an area to be grander than it actually is. Do your research before trusting an agency and also privately look up where they are sending you before agreeing to any terms. Their job is to fill vacancies, so once you are in country your contact with these agencies may be limited as well. Another issue that you may come across is since the agency is taking a fee from the school, this may actually come out of your pay. This may not seem like a big deal, but I have seen agencies take as much as 40% of what the teacher would have made if he or she was hired directly from the school. Just remember to be cautious whenever dealing with an agency and to NEVER give an agency or a school money or access to your bank account. It's sad to say but there are several scam artists out there trying to steal your money.

10 CURRICULUM VITAE

Having a properly formatted curriculum vita is the most important step in finding a job as an English teacher overseas. This is the first impression an employer will have of you and you want it to be a positive one. The format for a teaching position will be similar to that of other CVs but does have its own personal traits.

Your heading should stand alone and include your personal information. Make sure to include your address in this section. The employer will see this and will have an idea of whether you are a native speaker or not. Some employers are solely looking for native speakers and others are open to speakers of English as a second language. An address in a native speaking country will actually increase your odds of being hired, but if you have a local address you should include that as well. Your heading should also include your phone number, email address, and Skype ID. Majority of employers will contact you via email, but some prefer to speak over the phone. Also, if you have your Skype ID already on your CV, then when the employer requests a Skype interview, you can reference your CV, which will keep it in continual reference in the employers mind.

Example:

PATRICIA MUFFET

1025 Dreary Lane Brisbane, OH United Kingdom | +020 867 5309 | satonhertuffet@fairytale.com Skype ID- Miss Muffet

Next you should have a summary. The summary should be a brief description of the status of your career. You may reference your prior experience or career field or simply state what your position is that you are searching for or currently have.

Example:

SUMMARY

Early career educator traveling the world. Focus on secondary and adult education in multiple subjects.

Education is primarily the next section you should

address in your CV. You should make sure to include name of the university, type of degree, area of concentration, and any extra curricular activities you were involved with or positions you may have held. To the right include either your enrollment or graduation year.

If you have some college, I would still reference it in your CV. But, if you have not attended university, do not reference your secondary school under education. Stress your prior work experience and your certifications in lieu of your education. A degree is not required in many places to be a TEFL teacher, so do not stress if your CV shows limited education. Win them over with your other qualifications and your cover letter.

Example:

EDUCATION
  School of Hard Knocks
  B.S. in Science
   Areas of Concentration: Animal Husbandry
  Member of Ice Cream Donors Anonymous
  President of the Laser Tag Association

The next section should encompass any certifications that you may have. These can range from teaching certificates attached to your degree to any relevant certificate or award that you feel should be included in your CV. This is also where you should have what type of TEFL or CELTA certificate you have. Now, a TEFL or CELTA certificate is not required, but almost every employer is going to ask about this. If you do not have experience teaching, most will require you to get one. It is all right to apply while taking your TEFL certificate course and just write pending next to it on your CV. The schools will only need to see it upon arrival.

Example:

CERTIFICATION

Florida Teaching Certificate: 6-12 Social Sciences
TEFL Certificate: www.teachenglish.com (not a real website)
CELTA Certificate: Cambridge University

The next section of your CV that you need to include is experience. The more relevant experience you have to teaching the better, but we all have to start somewhere. If you are a recent graduate or new to the field of education, do not worry. There are several people in your shoes and many of the schools overseas are not worried about extensive experience in the field. Some jobs may require teaching experience, so you may have to build your resume by going to different countries before applying to that particular job.

If you have never taught before and have no idea what to put in the experience section, try to think of times where you had to instruct someone or give directions. Try to put anything that shows responsibility, planning skills, and ability to give instructions. Most schools understand that there are first year teachers and are still willing to hire them. As long as you have a TEFL or CELTA certificate and are a native speaker, you should have no problem finding a job regardless of your work experience.

Example:

EXPERIENCE

Small Town Paper Company
Manchester, New York Australia
Sales Manager   **2009**
Oversaw twenty-seven employees.
In charge of scheduling and delegating tasks.

University of Florida English Language Institute
Gainesville, FL USA
Language Assistant   **2014**
Created daily lesson plans for low-advanced students. Taught lessons in advanced listening and speaking course. Developed students conversation skills.

Other sections

You might consider adding an additional section or two if you have any other skills or accomplishments that you would like to mention. If you have published any writings, adding a listing is always a good way to strengthen your CV. Also, any awards that you may have won that are not mentioned in the education section could make a good section. Extra curricular activities and positions could also be added here if it is not already referenced earlier. A foreign language section is also a plus for applying for jobs abroad. Mention whether you took formal lessons or self taught. This shows that you have experience in a foreign language classroom and can understand the students' perspective. Regardless of what section you add here, make sure it individualizes you and helps you stand apart from the rest.

SAMPLE CV

PATRICIA MUFFET

1025 Dreary Lane Brisbane, OH United Kingdom
| +020 867 5309 | satonhertuffet@fairytale.com
SkypeID- Miss Muffet

SUMMARY

Early career educator traveling the world. Focus on secondary and adult education in multiple subjects.

EDUCATION

School of Hard Knocks
B.S. in Science
Areas of Concentration: Animal Husbandry
Member of Ice Cream Donors Anonymous
President of the Laser Tag Association

CERTIFICATION

Florida Teaching Certificate: 6-12 Social Sciences
TEFL Certificate: www.teachenglish.com (not a real website)
CELTA Certificate: Cambridge University

EXPERIENCE

Small Town Paper Company
Manchester, New York Australia
Sales Manager   **2009**
Oversaw twenty-seven employees.
In charge of scheduling and delegating tasks.

University of Florida English Language Institute
Gainesville, FL USA
Language Assistant   **2014**
Created daily lesson plans for low-advanced
students. Taught lessons in advanced listening
and speaking course.

11 COVER LETTER

A cover letter is your selling point to a company or school. This is where you give insight into who you are and why you want to come to their country. You should begin with a short backstory on yourself and tie in some of your experience. Do not make an annotated CV. In other words, do not just repeat all the information that they can get in your CV, make this more personal.

A good point of emphasis to put into your cover letter is why you want to go to their country and why you want to teach. Talk about places you want to see and parts of their culture you want to experience. If you have a little anecdote that ties their country into part of your life, use it, they will enjoy hearing that their country means so much to you. Make sure to mention your desire to be an educator and what kind of educator you are or plan to be. Some schools prefer strict teachers whereas others prefer fun and light-hearted teachers. Make sure to specify this part according to what kind of school you are applying to. The country that the school is in will also play a part in how they view education. Do some light research about the country, school, and education system before writing your cover letter.

Most importantly remember to represent yourself in the truest fashion. This is the initial sample portrayal of you before meeting them via Skype or other medium. Do not make yourself out to be something you are not. You do not want to pretend you are someone else your entire time in a new country, and they do not want to be getting a different person than the one they thought they hired. Just remember when writing your cover letter to put yourself in their shoes and ask yourself, "Would I hire this person?" As long as you speak from the heart and show them that this is what you want to do, you will most likely get a request for an interview.

12 PREPARING FOR THE INTERVIEW

After getting your name out there and sending your CV to possible employers you will start getting requests for interviews. If you applied from your home country or from a different country than the job is in, then the majority of schools will want to do this via Skype. You will get the rare request for a phone interview, I have mostly gotten these from schools in Korea or China, it is odd and make sure to research these schools twice over since majority of schools tend to interview through face time. Do make sure to dress as if you were doing the interview in person if it is conducted via Skype and present yourself in a professional manner.

If you are in country, treat the interview as you would any other job interview. Dress professionally, be well groomed, and prepared. Carry copies of your CV, even if you have given the company one previously. Sometimes more than one person will interview you and it is good for each of them to have a copy for reference.

A typical interview will take around an hour and is rather informal. The interviewer's job is to make sure that you speak clearly and will be able to handle the job they require. If you prepare for the interview, present yourself well, and remember that you are what they need then you will do fine. Almost every interview begins with a few "get to know you" questions. This is your chance to show who you are and what kind of personality they can expect from their possible future teacher. During this process of introductory questions they will probably ask you some personal questions on how you relate to cultures outside of your own. These questions are typically asked to make sure that you are comfortable living abroad in a new culture for an extended period of time.

Common questions or topics that come up in an interview are:

"Why do you want to come to our country?"

"What are your experiences with our culture?"

"What are your experiences outside of your own country/culture?"

In some cases like in Russia for instance you may be asked:

"How do you feel about the current political relations of our countries?"

Always talk up the country you plan on moving to. The interviewers love to hear how much you love their country and culture and how you want to see and learn more about them. They will also ask you a few cultural difference questions to see how you feel about being in a different culture. This is most common when speaking to countries that have a different common religion or vastly different culture than that of the Western world. As long as you show that the religious and cultural differences are not a problem for you and that you are actually excited about the possibility of experiencing them, then the interviewer will be satisfied and you will have passed their test.

Majority of schools will also give you curriculum and classroom behavior based questions. They will give you scenarios and ask how you would react or how you would teach a certain lesson. When it comes to classroom behavior questions, always say that you will report it to your superior and allow them to decide what should be done. You are going to be an outsider in their school and it is always best to leave any disciplinary action to your superiors. In any scenario that is uncommon to you, ask questions on what are the proper steps to rectify said situation. Try not to take things into your own hands; it rarely ends in your favor.

When it comes to curriculum-based questions, it is all right to hesitate for a moment and think about your answer. If you have already finished your TEFL certificate, then you will have gone over most of these situations or teaching questions before; simply just review what you have learned and recite it back to them. If you have not finished the TEFL certificate or have not started it yet, then it is best for you to research common TEFL lesson plans. Try and decide based on how you want to teach and the culture you are going to be living in, what kind of teacher are you going to be? Are you going to be a fun energetic teacher with lots of games or more of a strict teacher that has a more serious classroom setting? I try to be a mix of both. I am outgoing in my classroom, but I am also demanding of my students. This is what they are looking for in your answer. How are you going to conduct your class and do you know what you are doing? Now, do not let this make you nervous if you are a first time teacher. Think back to a classroom setting and a teaching style that worked well for you as a student and try to emulate your answer on how that teacher would have taught the lesson. You will also be given curriculum training when you do your TEFL certificate.

Here are some examples of a couple common curriculum questions you may receive:

"How would you teach prepositions to children 8-10 years old?"

> -There are typically one or two situational questions like this. Your TEFL certificate will prepare you to answer these questions.

"What do you tend to focus on in your lessons?"

> -i.e. listening, speaking, grammar, etc. I personally focus on speaking but I make sure to let my employer know that I still make sure to cover grammar.

"What are your feelings about homework?"

> -Some countries expect different amounts of homework to be given. Some prefer little, whereas others demand quite a bit. It would be a good idea to do some research on this subject and be flexible in your answer.

13 QUESTIONS TO ASK THE EMPLOYER

Towards the end of the interview, the interviewer will typically ask if you have any questions for them. It is good to have a list of questions prepared. Some of these questions may have already been addressed during the interview, but there may be some information that is best to get now instead of later through email. Myself, I like to have the list in front of me during the interview, and during the interview fill in the information provided. You might think that continually writing during an interview might seem rude, but in actuality it shows that you are prepared, you know what you are looking for in an employer, and that you have options that you are going to compare. The employer is taking notes down about you; it is only logical to do the same about the employer.

Salary

The first thing you should address is salary. It may feel uncomfortable to begin by discussing your income, but it is by far the most important topic. Unless you can afford to support yourself on your savings and are doing this for the experience, then this is impossible without a sufficient income. First you should ask if your income is going to be salary or hourly based. Most schools will pay salary. Is your pay going to be bi-weekly or monthly? This will help you budget your money by knowing how often you will be receiving a paycheck. You should also ask how many hours you will be working. This is not only something you should ask if you are being paid by the hour but also for salary jobs as well. You don't want to end up taking a job that seems like it pays well, but it ends up requiring you to teach fifty plus hours a week. A typical teacher with a full load should teach between twenty and twenty-five hours a week. Don't forget you have to spend time preparing for your classes and grading as well.

Housing

The next item that you need to address is housing. Many schools out there will give housing assistance.

They will either offer a certain allowance on top of your salary that they will put towards a residence of your choosing or some will provide an apartment or flat themselves for you to reside. If the school hires many native speakers then you may have an option of having a roommate. These places are typically bigger, but I would ask if it was all right if you met your potential abode dweller before deciding.

If they do not provide housing, simply mark it down and move on to the next topic. Later you will want to price check how much housing typically costs and do a cost analysis of it compared to your income. Sometimes it doesn't make much of a difference. A lot of times the schools that provide housing take it into consideration when making your salary offer and deduct it accordingly. At a later time, if you decide on a school that doesn't provide housing, you should ask about places to rent that are relatively close to the school.

Location

This is where the question of transportation comes into play. If they provide housing, ask how close to the school it is and if they could provide you with the name of the place or neighborhood so you can check it out. At least ask to see some pictures, you would be surprised what some schools think is suitable living for a teacher. Once you know the relativity of your place to the school, you should ask about public transport. Some people get a vehicle while living abroad, which can be a good or a bad thing. I had a motorbike in Asia and I was very glad I had one, but the public transportation system in the city I was living was unpredictable and quite expensive if used on a consistent basis. Yet in some countries, having a vehicle is not needed, especially in large cities. Most everything may be within walking distance or a cheap ride on public transportation. This is something you need to address with your employer. Simply ask them, "How is transportation in your city?"

Flight Reimbursement

The next subject you need to cover with your employer is flight reimbursement. This is typical for jobs that you set up in advance. Some schools will reimburse your plane ticket up to a certain amount which if you shopped around for your ticket properly then you will have no problem being under the spread. It is typical for you to be able to get your ticket reimbursement in the form of another ticket. You can use this ticket to visit home for the holidays or go on a vacation or return home after your contract is complete. Another option that some schools offer is that instead of a ticket you can exchange it for a lump sum of cash. Some times this is the best bet, especially if you are nifty at getting deals on flights. Not every school offers this incentive, but a lot do so it never hurts to ask.

Health Insurance

The next thing you should ask is if the school provides health insurance. If you already have health insurance you should check to see if it covers you overseas, but many schools or countries will provide health insurance. In some countries it's really not needed because the cost of health care is so low. In Thailand, I was treated for Dengue Fever for around twenty-one dollars. Granted there wasn't a cure and it was mostly blood work, doctor visits, and prescriptions; but hey it was still very cheap. In any case, it's always a good idea to ask if they provide any coverage or if the government requires any coverage. In Europe, it is mandatory to have health insurance if you are a working immigrant: still relatively cheap.

One of the most important things you need to ask about is your work visa. Make sure to ask about the process, whether it needs to be handled prior to your flight or when you are in country, if you have to pay for it or will the school be handling payment, and how much assistance is the school going to provide in the process. This is the most important part of working outside of your country. This is what makes you legal. You don't want to blow this off and a few months into your stay get deported and be forever marked as an illegal worker. Make the employer go into detail about how and what you need to do for your visa and make sure to ask if they are going to help you. You would be surprised how many immigration offices do not speak English and will just send you in circles. The more assistance you have, the easier the immigration process will be. You will gain a new found respect for immigrants once you become one and have to go through processing. Be diligent with a school and do not let up when it comes to your work visa.

14 WEIGH YOUR OPTIONS

Make sure to take several interviews. A job may seem perfect, but there might still be a better option out there. It is always a good idea to have several options, so you can compare and contrast them to decide which is going to be the best for you. It is also quite exciting if they are in different parts of the world. Just imagine yourself in each of these places. No matter where you go, you will have an amazing time as long as you are open to immersing yourself in the country and do as much as you can. This is the time to decide what it is that you are looking for. Whether it be living on the beach in Central or South America or the big city life of a large Asian city or living in the countryside of an Eastern European city. The world is your oyster and now you are getting concrete options for the location of your next great adventure. And it will be an adventure, I promise you. Take this decision seriously as well. Look into the political situations, possible disease outbreaks, natural disasters, or any other dangers that might accompany a particular country. A country might sound like a great option, but its current status might make it one to put on the back burner for another time. Stay current with world news and use it as a tool to help you make your decision. You are committing to a school for an extended period of time and you need to be prepared to handle what that entails. This does not mean that if something happens it is not all right to change your mind and go home, but when a company hires you, they expect you to be there for the entirety of the contract and are put in a difficult situation if you do not follow through with your obligations. So, be prepared to commit and be absolutely positive this is what you want before you agree to take a position at a school.

15 I HAVE PICKED A JOB AND COMMITTED, NOW WHAT?

Contract

The first thing you want to do is request a copy of the contract. This will give you an opportunity to go through the contract and address any discrepancies. Having a copy of the contract also gives you legitimacy of employment. If a school is hesitant to give send you a copy of the contract then you should in turn be weary of accepting an offer from them. There are many scams out there and false employers, so be careful and be diligent in your research of a company or school. If you found the job on a trustworthy website then you should not have to worry, but it is always better to be thorough and be sure that you are signing a contract with a legitimate employer.

Visa

Next you should find out if you can begin working on the visa process. Some countries will allow you to start putting in paperwork for a work visa prior to your arrival, while others require you to do the processing in country. Remember some countries will not allow you to enter without a visa. This is one of the most important things to handle when moving to another country, so do not waste time. The sooner you have your visa processed the sooner you no longer have to deal with the bureaucracy.

There are a few countries that will require you to do a "border run" in order to get the work permit. This is actually quite common. Now there are two different types of "border runs": the tourist visa run and the work visa run. The tourist visa run is for when a person only has a tourist visa for a country and the visa is about to expire. That person will travel to a bordering country and then return with a new tourist visa that will be valid for an extended period of time. If you work with only a tourist visa, you are working illegally and can be prosecuted. I would not suggest doing this. It is easy enough to get a work visa and if a company or school does not sponsor you for one then you should consider working for someone else. Constantly doing border runs is not worth the risk. A work visa run is for someone who has a tourist visa for a country and the country does not allow immigrants to process a work visa within their borders. So the person must go to a neighboring country and go to the embassy of the country they would like to have a work permit in and do the processing there. Make sure that you have all of your paperwork in line and are prepared for processing. In some countries they will speak very little English and it can be quite difficult. Ask your company or school for assistance and have them go over all of the visa requirements with you. If at all possible, see if they can send someone to assist you at the embassy. One other tip while on a visa run: sometimes you will see people outside of the embassy offering to do the paperwork for you for a fee, do not let them. Most likely they are using the wrong paperwork and will steal your identity. This is a scam and a waste of money. You can do the paperwork yourself, and if you need help, someone in the embassy will be able to assist you. Visa runs can be confusing and exhausting, so it is best to have everything in line if you have to do one, that way you only have to do it once.

You can also get visa information from your government's site.

Example for Americans:

travel.state.gov

Or websites like **projectvisa.com** can provide more

information.

Airfare

If you are required to provide your own initial airfare, it is a good idea to get a jump on booking it as soon as you are able. Doing an extensive search is the best route in finding a ticket for a reasonable or even cheap price. Don't just go directly to the airline or the most well known travel sites and book the first ticket you see. I would spend a few days and look into as many different airfare sites as you can. Also play around with the dates of departure in order to find the best deal. You would be surprised on the difference in price of simply booking on different days of the week. Give yourself a window of dates that you would like to leave that still leave you at least a few days prior to the beginning of your contract to depart. You will want the time to adjust to the jetlag and adapt to your new surroundings before beginning work. Another option in booking is finding airfares with an extended layover, perhaps a day or two. These tickets can be cheaper and also give you the opportunity to check out another country during your travel. I had an extended layover in the Emirates and was able to see Abu Dhabi; a city I might never had been able to see otherwise. Also look into flying into and from different cities than the direct route. The fares may be cheaper if you leave from a city that might have more frequent flights in the direction you are headed. Also landing in a nearby airport that has more international flights may also make the price of the flight less expensive. The cost of taking another form of transport from a different city to your final destination may be less than flying direct.

Finances

If possible you should save as much as you can prior to leaving. You will have some upfront costs in the beginning and it may take roughly a month or so before your first paycheck. Now, I am not saying that you need to arrive with a bankroll or must have a lot of money to be able to do this, but having emergency funds is always a good option. Put away a little each month to help you with your initial costs of airfare, housing, visas, and other necessities that you will need upon arrival. I have gone overseas financially unprepared and found it struggling and was not able to do all the things that I wanted to do. If you come with some savings, you will be able to do some exploring and it will make your transition into your new life less stressful if you do not have to worry about money. After checking the cost of living, look into how much an average apartment is, the cost of a visa, and the average prices of other expenses. This will give you a rough estimate of how much you should try and save prior to leaving. I will have some money saving tips in a further section on arrival in the new country.

16 LEARN AS MUCH ABOUT THE COUNTRY AS YOU CAN

It is always a good idea to get to learn as much about the country you are moving to as you can. The more you know, the better prepared you are for the transition and it's also good for conversation if you know things about their country and can reference things that they know. You will get asked a lot about your own country, but if you show an interest in theirs as well, it will go a long way.

History

Learning a bit of a country's history will help you understand why certain things are the way they are. You will be able to understand what certain things, like monuments, are and what their importance is. Now you don't have to be a historian about the country, but maybe read a few articles about the history of the nation. It will make sight seeing more meaningful and people will appreciate the fact that you know some details about their history. If you do want to go into more detail into the country's history, there are several books that encompass any country or regions history. There is a collection called "The Concise History of *(insert name of country here)* that does a very good job in their historiographies.

Watching films that take place in the country that have historical or cultural references is a good window to a country. Make sure the movies are relatively accurate. So in other words don't watch *The Italian Job* to get a frame of reference about Italy or *The Hangover II* to learn about Thailand. If you have the opportunity, try and find some films and music that were created by the people of the country. It will give insight into how people are and people love it when you can make cultural references that they can relate to. Either way, knowing where a people have been will help you understand where they are now and where they are going

Politics

You should also look into the current political situation. Know what type of government the country has and who its top leaders are, at least the president, prime minister, or king. Read into any political discrepancies of the past decade. Try to have a general idea of what is going on in politics and what are the most important issues to the people. Normally, people don't talk politics with foreigners but it is a good subject for debate in your classroom. It is also good to have an idea of what are hot button topics with people and to know what is going on in government because it may affect you. While I was in Thailand, the General of the Army took over the government and changed some of the immigration rules, and I had to be aware of the new system in order to be able to stay in the country. The more you understand about what is going on, the better prepared you are for what could happen.

Geography

You should also look into the geography of the country and region. It is not only beneficial for knowing where places that you might want to visit are in relation to you, but you will be able to understand references and when talking to people about local travel or where they are from, you will know what they are talking about. You would be surprised how excited people get when you know where a place is that isn't commonly known globally. Think about being abroad and when you tell people where you are from; if you are not from a major city, then you will use a different better-known municipality for reference. Now, imagine if someone knows about your hometown, you get excited and want to talk about it. This is the same with people you will meet abroad. Don't think you need to be a cartographer of the region before arrival, just have a general understanding of the region, you will understand the local geography much better once you spend some time in the country and region.

Sightseeing

You should also look up what the major tourist attractions, national parks, and historical sites are and where they will be in relation to you. This is one of the exciting parts of preparation, you start to get a visual of things you will see on this adventure and can start making plans to go see the places that interest you the most. You can also check what the local attractions in your city are and see what your new home is going to look like. You will also have a reference of things to do during your time off and be able to ask locals which are worthwhile and which are a waste of time. Locals are normally really honest when it comes to attractions in their city and will let you know if it is worth doing. Some attractions are for "tourists" only and if you want to be part of the locality, if they appose a place then you follow suit. You may still want to check our the "tourist" spots, but make sure not to bring it up around the locals, especially if it is a place they do not support for example some zoos or wildlife parks might not have local support.

Culture

An important thing to research is the dos and don'ts in a culture. It is really easy to offend or anger someone accidentally without even realizing that you are doing something wrong. There are things that you do in your culture that are no big deal that are major social faux pas. Whether it be pointing your feet at someone or touching their head in Southeast Asia or using your left hand or giving the thumbs up in parts of the Middle East or the OK sign in Brazil or holding out your palm like for a high five in Greece or chewing gum in Singapore. So many things that you might consider innocent gestures are taken as a major insult in other parts of the world and are good to know in advance before accidentally upsetting people. You should also know what is considered polite, like how to bow in different parts of Asia. The appropriateness of cheek kisses is something that differs quite a lot from country to country. Just do your best to not offend people, but most people understand that you are foreign and are quite forgiving if you make a mistake; but not always, so it is best to know how to avoid offending people and prevent any possible confrontations.

You should also look into the regions typical attitudes towards race, gender, religion, and sexuality. Some cultures might not be as tolerant as you might expect. In some countries it could be actively dangerous for you. In larger international cities this might not be an issue, but it is a very important thing to look into. I have been offended countless times due to being in regions that had a different point of view than my own. Remember you are staying in this place for an extended period of time, you do not want to live in a place where you are in danger or will experience prejudice on a daily basis.

Language

Another helpful thing you can do to prepare yourself for living in a new country is learning some basic phrases. I am not saying that you need to speak a language fluently before going there, but being able to say a few phrases never hurt. I would at least learn basic greetings, "how much", numbers, "yes" and "no", "do you speak English?", and maybe a few other phrases that you might find helpful. I didn't prepare enough when I went to Thailand and for the first couple of days I was walking around saying "wai", which means to bow, instead of saying the proper greeting for hello. Imagine if someone walked up to you, bowed, and then said, "to bow." You would think this person is very strange and believe me people did. Thankfully someone on the subway instructed me in the proper greeting, but if I had learned it before getting to the country, I could have saved myself a lot of embarrassment.

Conversion Ratio

Learning the conversion ratio or at least a quick formula is always a good idea. It will put what you are spending into terms that you understand, especially in countries with great inflation. When I was in Laos the conversion ratio was around 8,000 kip to the US dollar. Purchasing things became very confusing and sometimes I did not know if I was spending a lot of money or not. You should also take into consideration the cost of living and your salary when converting money. Find a common item like a can of Coke or a sandwich and think when you are purchasing something, "OK, that is worth 7 sandwiches, is it worth it?" By comparing it to a common purchase, you understand what value the vendor is putting on an item and you can determine if your values are equal. Another good tool is to compare it to your salary. First, figure out what your hourly wage and use it in comparison to the object, "OK, I have to work two and a half hours for this, is it worth it?" This is literally treating time as money, which as a teacher you are selling your time, so it is equal to money. For large purchases I suggest comparing it to your total monthly income. If something cost half your monthly income, it better be worth it.

Cost of Living

Researching the cost of living is something you should do as well. You should have done this already to see if your salary is comparable to where you are going to live. This way you can create a budget and know how much you will have for a disposable income. You don't want to get to a country and your salary is just enough to get by. This will make the living overseas unbearable. You want to make sure you have enough to go and do things and be able to see as much as you can. By making a general budget life will be much easier and you will get more out of the experience. This is something that you can gain a general understanding of prior to getting there, but it will be easier to determine once you are living in the country and have a feel for what things cost and build your routine.

You will adapt to your new surroundings once you get to the country, but it never hurts to be a little prepared. You don't have to be an expert on everything about the country and culture. This is impossible, unless you spend years studying and even then you will never fully grasp all there is about a place until you live there. Just try to learn what you can in advance to give yourself a leg up and make your transition easier. It is an amazing feeling to have things you have read about come to life before your eyes. The more you know about where you are going

the easier it is to hit the ground running. Arriving
without knowing anything will leave you in complete
disarray.

17 HOW TO PACK

Majority of contracts are at least six months to a year, so you may be inclined to bring with you as much as possible. I cannot stress enough how bad of an idea this is. There is nothing worse than trying to get around in a foreign country with an over abundance of baggage. Pack light and to climate. The best way to pack for an extended stay overseas is to pack as if it were a two-week business trip. You should bring professional style clothes for work. If you are a man this means nice slacks, dress shirts, ties, and a sports coat if possible. If you are a woman, I would look up what is considered professional dress in the country you are moving to. The appropriate feminine attire can vary greatly from region to region. You should also bring with you a few casual outfits as well.

If you are moving to a country with varied

seasons. Pack for the weather that will be in effect immediately upon arrival. It is typically cheaper and more convenient to buy a winter coat or whatever seasonal clothing you may require than it is to bring with you clothes for every season. If you are style conscious this could also be an issue, because what is trendy in one part of the world may differ from another.

Do not load down your luggage with toiletries, blankets, pillows, towels, and other unnecessary items. You can purchase these items in the new country and typically at a low cost. If you have room in you luggage, bringing a single lightweight towel would not be a bad idea. You may have to stay in a hotel or hostel your first couple days, so having your own towel might be necessary, this also depends on where you are moving. One item that is extremely handy is a wattage converter. All around the world you will find that the plugs are different shapes and wattage. Having a wattage converter allows you to use your electronical devices abroad. These are relatively inexpensive and can be a "life-saver" in a new country. Other than similar lightweight necessities, do not over pack.

If you are an avid reader, like myself, you might be inclined to bring a small "library" with you. I would suggest bringing a few books along for the ride, but once again, do not weigh yourself down with too many items. At most carry with you 3-5 books, at the absolute most. You will be able to find books in English or be able to order from a local source online, these options are much cheaper and more convenient than toting around several books. A Kindle might also be a wise purchase to reduce the weight and still be able to bring your books with you.

Make sure to bring some sort of entertainment with you. If you are a reader this means a couple books, but if not try to find something that you enjoy that is lightweight and easily transportable. Depending on where you are going, you might have a bit of a journey, and it is better to have something to occupy your attention than to spend countless hours of staring out a window. Also, you might not have internet access right away, so having something will also keep you from being bored when you first move to your new home. Upload a couple movies to your computer or a game or anything that will allow you some form of entertainment while you are at home. It is nice to have a piece of home and normality when you are thrown into a whirlwind of change. Believe me, you will end up missing the most trivial of things, even things that you were not to keen on back home will become longing. Having a book or movie in your own native language can mean the world when you are far from home.

18 I HAVE ARRIVED

You have arrived at your new home abroad. You are probably excited and want to start exploring right off the bat, but I suggest taking it easy the first day. You will be in this country for an extended period of time, so there is no need to try and see everything the first day. Take it easy your first day, go to a local restaurant and try a new cuisine, and just relax. Jetlag is a real thing and depending on how far away you are moving can seriously throw your body through a loop. Try to go to bed at a reasonable hour the first night to allow your body to adjust to the new time zone. It won't happen overnight but the quicker you try to adjust the quicker you will, but don't be surprised if you end up a night owl if you end up moving East.

After resting up the first night, now it is time to explore. If you landed in the city that you are moving to then you might want to start setting up your living situation and visiting your new employer. But, if you have time, then take it to see this wonderful new place you will learn to call home. You will be able to do some exploring during the school year, but this will mainly be during national holidays and you might want to spend those with your new-found local friends.

Arriving in a country a few days or weeks before the start of your contract is a good idea. This gives you ample time to adjust to the jetlag and a chance to prepare yourself prior to beginning your job. You can take this time to see some of the country and take in the sights.. You will also be able to begin to understand some of the ways people act and start adjusting to the culture. This will be helpful, because, through trial and error, you will learn things about the people of the country that you don't want to just become aware of in the work place. You will also be able to make local references that you were not aware of prior in your classroom, and students tend to become more involved when you can make the class relevant to them.

If you are a drinker and a person who likes to party, now is the time to do so. You will still be able to go out and have fun once you are settled in, don't get me wrong, but depending on the type of school and your hours, you might be working early during the week and won't have the free time that you have now. Also, depending on the size of the new city you are moving to and the culture, it might not be a good idea to be going out drinking all the time if everyone knows that you are teaching their kids. If this is the case and you still want to party on weekends, do what I did and go to a neighboring city. You will get to check out somewhere new and not have the stigma of the drunken teacher.

If you arrived early, this is the time to be the tourist who gets to say, "yeah, I just moved here." Believe it or not, saying that you live there goes a long way with locals, and they are more inclined to show you around and be open to you. You are not to them just another foreigner passing through. You are a new local that they will want to show what it means to be a local. This is the best part of moving and working abroad. A tourist goes to a country and sees the sights and then leaves and goes "ah, that was nice." A TEFL teacher or anyone who lives in a country for an extended period of time gets to further understand a culture and will, at least in part, know what it is like to be a person from that country. You have the opportunity to be a "semi-local" and be part of the community.

When you do arrive and settle into your new city, try and be a part of the community. Go to local events, make local friends, learn something new, be one of them. You will gain so much more and enjoy your stay a thousand-fold if you are not a recluse and get out as much as you can and experience everything this new culture has to offer. You are there to teach, but you will learn so much more through your experiences than could ever be taught in a classroom.

19 COMMUNICATION

When it comes to communicating with friends or family back home, social media sites and other internet based communication is typically the best route. It is generally free and is easily accessible. The one issue you might have is internet access upon arrival, your apartment might not have it set up yet or, depending on the region, might not be available. Bring with you a couple of phone cards, just in case, this will guarantee you will have communication back home. There is the issue of your phone working in a new country. Typically you can buy a cheap prepaid SIM card and insert it into your preexisting phone and will have access. This is helpful because you will probably need to have a local number for your work to get in touch with you. If the SIM card does not work in your phone, you are left with two options. You can have the phone unlocked, but mind you this could void the warranty of the phone and in some cases not be legal. The other option is purchasing a phone in the new country. If this is your option, you can pick up a cheap old style phone in most places at a low cost. Newer phones though, can be quite expensive in certain countries, so it might benefit you to handle this issue prior to leaving, either by purchasing an international phone or discussing your options with your current carrier.

Depending on where you go, you might also find that there are restrictions to the internet and certain sites that you frequent back home are not available. **Bare in mind the following information may violate telecommunication laws in certain countries.** If you want your internet access to be the same as back home, many people use proxy servers. If you are unfamiliar with this term, a proxy server is basically a way to trick your computer into thinking it is on a different country's network. Do not waste money on purchasing a proxy server. There are plenty of free ones out there that work perfectly fine. You can simply type into a search engine "free proxy server" and several options will appear. Make sure to check reviews on the proxy server before using it. **Once again, this option may violate telecommunication laws in certain countries and is here for informational use. I in no way am suggesting or condone the use of proxy servers,**

but am just simply providing information.

20 FIRST DAY AT WORK

The first day you meet your employer dress a professional as possible. Make a good first impression. It is better to be overdressed than to look like you don't take the job seriously. You can adapt your dress to mimic the other teachers after you know what is appropriate attire and what is not. Present yourself in a formal manner and let the informalities come naturally. Remember you are here to work and as much as it might seem like an extended vacation, your employer expects a professional. I am not saying that you cannot be fun and personable, but test the water before plunging in with any extravagance.

In your first class, I suggest showing a bit of strictness with a bit of fun. These might seem like contradictory ideas, but in a classroom they are a must. If you have never been a teacher before, then think of your teachers that you learned the most from. Most likely they were entertaining, yet demanded respect. Try to emulate the teachers that made the greatest impression on you and you will do fine. If you have taught before, then you already understand what I am saying. The first class may be daunting, but remember they are terrified of you. They have been studying English and now they are presented with a native speaker. Try to ease the process, but do not let the students run the class.

Be prepared for your lesson. Most schools will have a curriculum or a guideline that they would like you to follow, but some will require you to create your own. If the school provides books, then this will be simple. Just follow along with the book and create a few exercises that correspond with the subject. But, if you are required to create your own, don't panic. Spend your first class getting to know the students and try to figure out their level of comprehension. It can be as simple as asking each student to introduce themselves and say a fact or two about their interests. Once you know their comprehension of the English language, you can find several lesson plans online to assist you in their understanding.

Focus on speaking and listening. You can do some work on grammar and you should, but you are a native speaker and for some of these students their only opportunity to speak with one. They will be hesitant to speak, so correct but make sure to allow some mistakes to slide. Always correct at the end. Allow the student to get through their thought process before being corrected, because the correction may deter them from wanting to continue and reduce their output.

You should always have a second lesson plan prepared. You might think you have an awesome lesson planned, but it might just not take with the students and instead of forcing something that they are completely struggling with have an alternate to save them and you the strife. I once tried teaching accents to an advanced group at a university in the United States and the students were simply not able to handle the lesson. Upon realizing this, I changed the subject matter and the class went on successfully; but if I did not have something else prepared, the class would have been a disaster and I would have spent an hour talking to blank faces.

So be prepared and take your job seriously. These students and your employer expect you to be a professional, and even if it is your first time, still try to act like you know what you are doing and do the best you can to teach your students. You and your students will benefit the most if you are serious about what you do and are gaining from the experience. There is nothing worse than going to a class where both the students and the teacher know that the other doesn't want to be there.

You will from time to time have the disruptive student. We all know this kid. He or she is the jokester who tries to be cool and in some cases can be a royal pain in the ass for the teacher. At first try and take this student to the side and ask why he or she is so disruptive. Do not try and make an example out of him or her or embarrass him or her in front of the class. If the student continues to be a distraction in the class, do not take matters into your own hands and try to discipline the student. Speak with your supervisor and have them handle it. In many cultures this is the best route since you are an outsider and they should handle the problem. You typically won't have this problem, but if you do it is best to bring it to their attention and allow the school administrators to handle it rather than to try and deal with it on your own.

21 NEW HOME

Teaching English in a new country can be both difficult and rewarding. Now I change countries every year and get to experience a life outside my own. Each new place a new adventure and a new me. I travel as a teacher, but I end up learning ten fold what I could ever teach in a classroom. I am able to grow as a person and take parts of each culture with me. My weekend getaways are to strange and new places that I never imagined were there. The world is my home now and I am thankful for it and it all began in that village in Thailand not so long ago.

.... We stop by a small building with a wooden bench outside. He tells me to sit down, as he walks over to a fridge pulls out a couple of bottles and hands the woman at the counter a few coins. He hands me the large beer. "Relax." I took a deep breath. "Wheeeew." We sat there and talked about the village

and where we were from and this, that, and the other.
We discussed his lesson plan that I would be taking
over and the students. Now I had something to focus
on, the students. My worries eased a bit.

A couple days later was my first day. The
students were in awe of me. They smiled
tremendously and shied away when I waved at them.
All of the anxiety I had felt was gone now. I was just
as much of a novelty for them as Thailand was for me.
Each day at the school, I fell more and more in love
with Thailand and Thai culture. My doubts and
inhibitions felt like a distant memory. I had no
problem calling this my new home.

ABOUT THE AUTHOR

David Zelnar is from Islamorada, Florida. He studied history at the University of Florida. He began his teaching career as a Language Assistant at the University of Florida's English Language Institute. From there he taught English as a Second Language in Thailand and in Poland. He is currently still teaching and working on his writing career.

Made in the USA
Lexington, KY
29 November 2018